EXCUSE ME DAD, WHAT ARE WE?

ADAM DAWSON

First edition May 2023

Illustrations generated using DALL-E
Book design by Virtual Painbrush Book Design

ISBN 978-0-6458175-0-8 (hardcover)
ISBN 978-0-6458175-1-5 (paperback)
ISBN 978-0-6458175-2-2 (ebook)

DEDICATED TO

Maxwell and Oscar

WE ARE PART OF of an **8.1 billion** strong group of humans currently living, in **195 different countries**, speaking about **7000 different languages**, on the planet **Earth** in **2023**.

We are part of **all the lifeforms** that have ever existed on this planet over the last **3.5 billion years**.

We are connected to **all life** on Earth because we have **the same needs**.

All life must **balance** the combination of **two different energies**,

the **female** and the **male**.

All life must **absorb the sun**, **drink water**, and **digest nutrients** to survive.

We are **flying through space** on our planet at **220 kilometres per second**, following and orbiting our sun. We're also spinning at **1670 kilometres per hour**.

When feeling **uneasy**, it helps to physically ground ourselves in **balanced positions**.

The brain is processing **thousands** of impulses every second.

The human brain is built
to **keep getting better**.

For **99.9%** of our time on Earth, humans were living **quite differently** to how we live now. There was a lot of suffering in the past. In **2023** there are still **many people living poorly**.

Computers and phones are relatively new, even cars are quite new. We are **still learning** how to best use them. The world is changing very quickly these days, but that hasn't always been the case.

Many of the things that are normal for you, are **miracles** for old people.

Now is the **safest it has ever been** to grow up on Earth, we enjoy **higher wellbeing** than any of our ancestors.

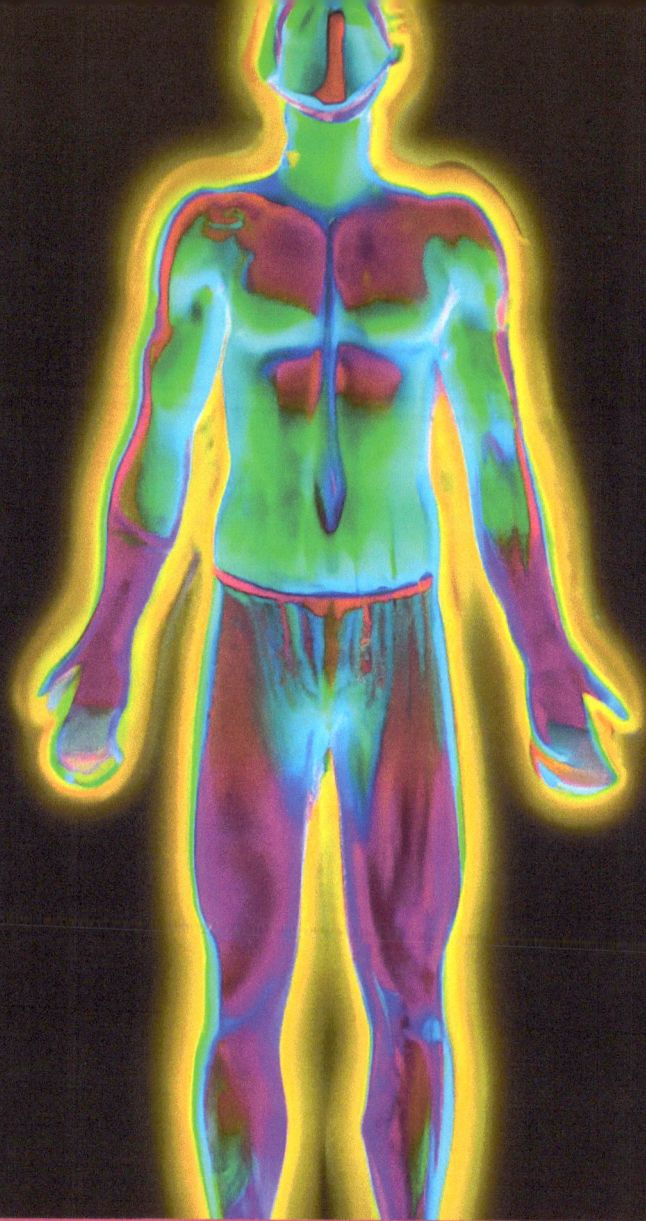

Every human's body is radiating a **bio-electric magnetic energy field** that is caused by our inner functions — our **brain activity**, our **heart pumping blood through our veins**, and our **lungs expanding and contracting**.

We **benefit** when our **energy field combines** with other humans.

Our energy comes from the **food** we put in our bodies.
Protein, **vitamins** and **minerals** produce **high energy**.

Energy is always **flowing through us**.
We can direct it however we like.

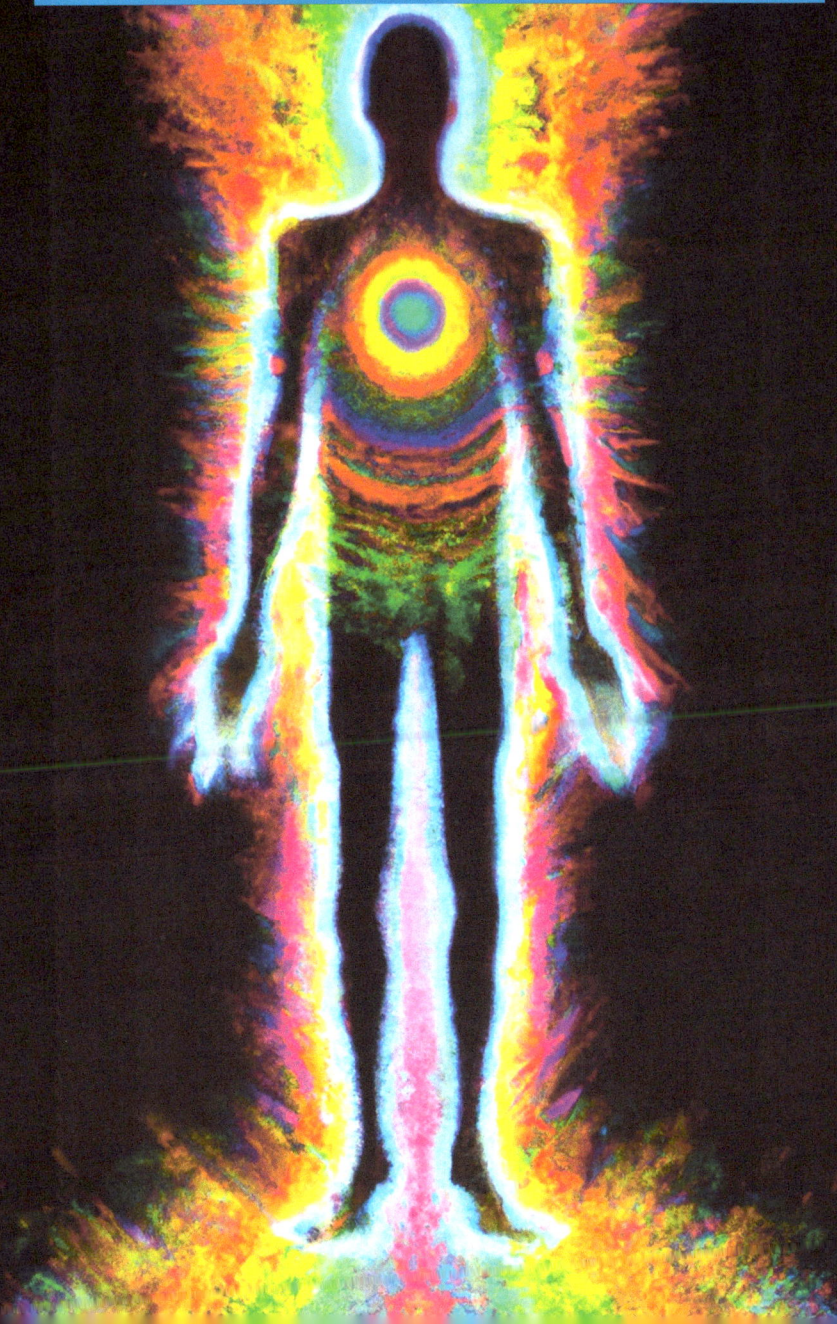

Our **growth** is determined by our **environment** and our **frame of mind**. Both types of stimuli affect how we grow.

Positive thoughts prepare us for growth.

Regularly give your body time, in **quiet stillness**. Equally as regularly, give your body time to **practice moving**.

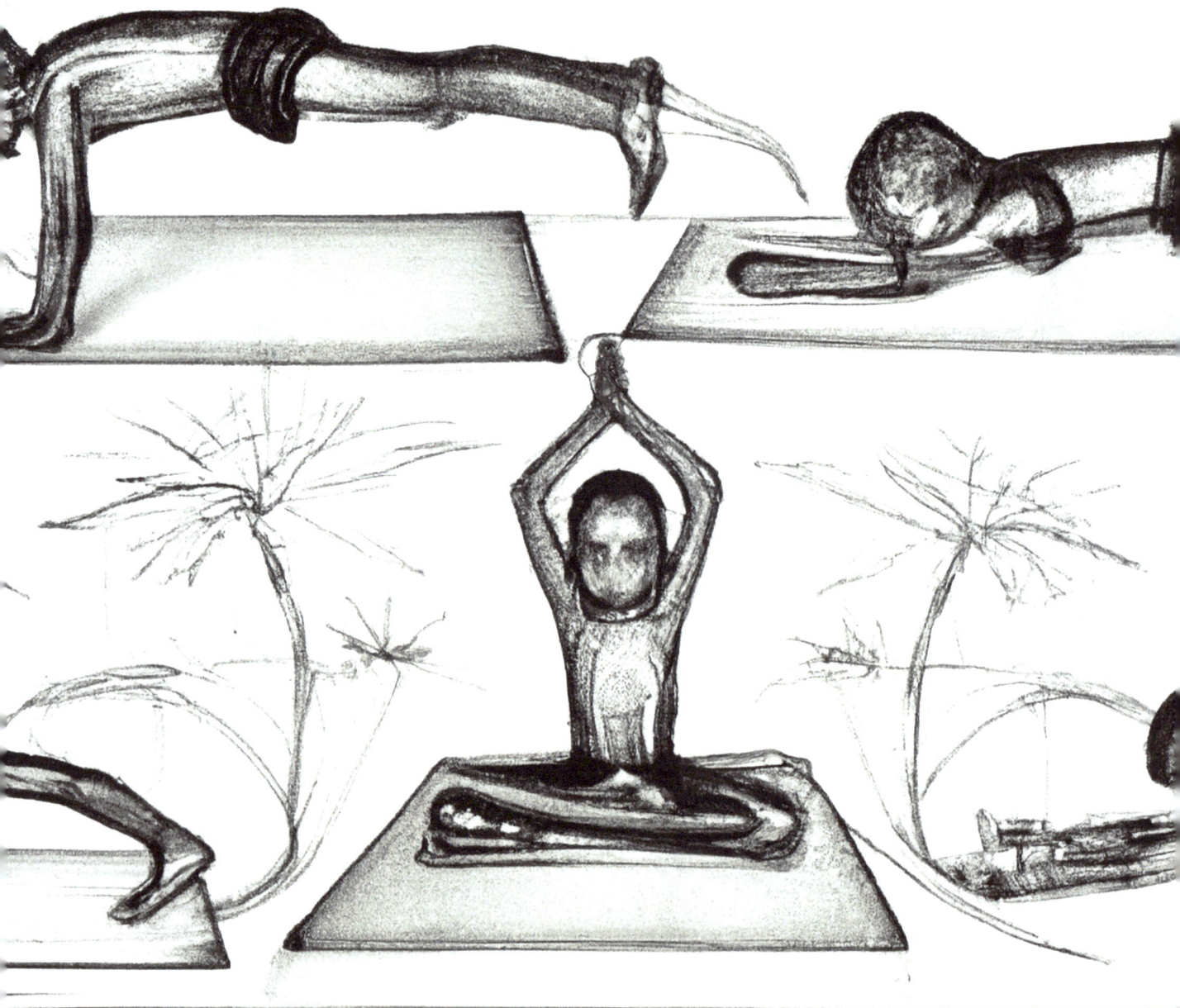

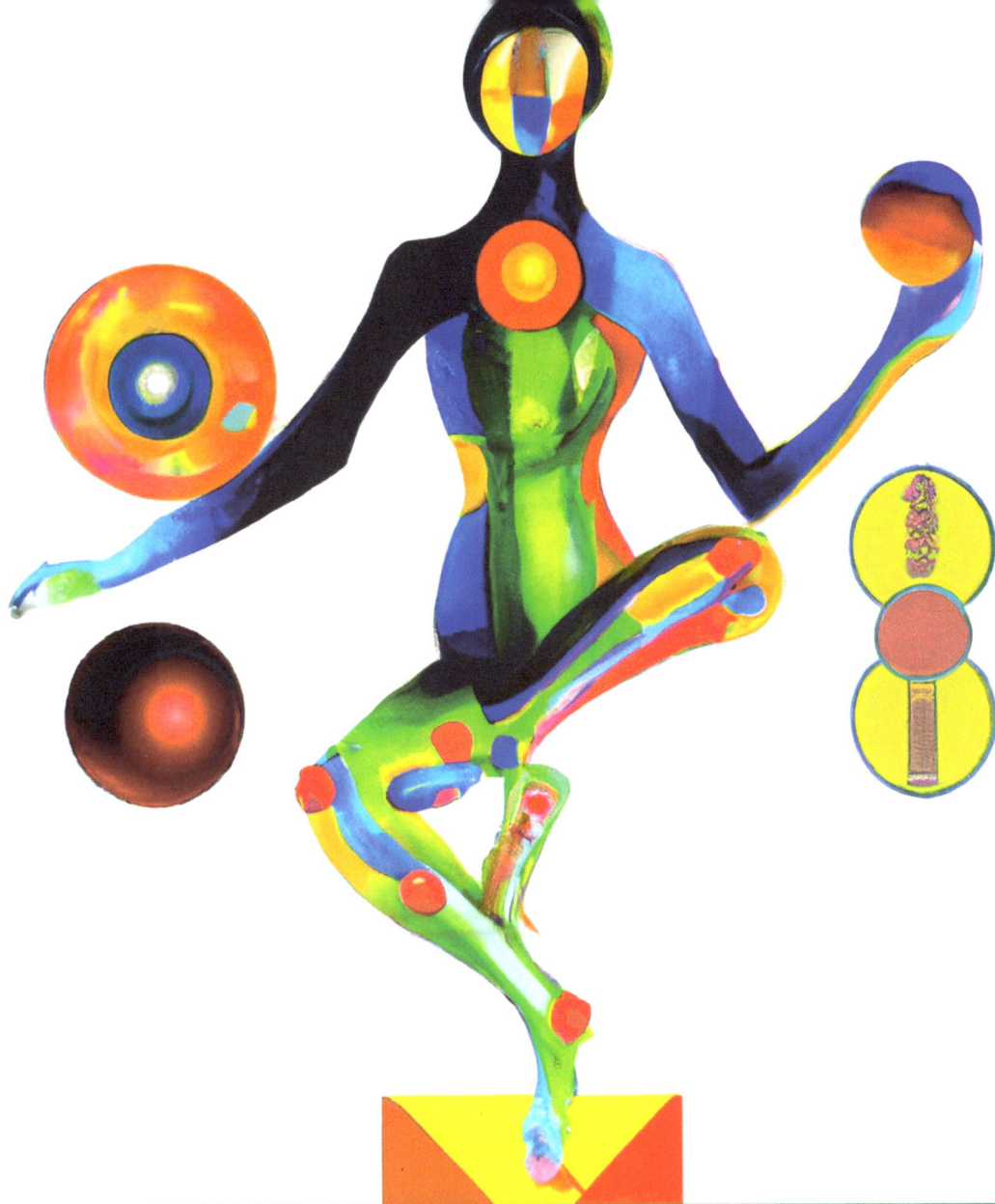

Balance female and male energy in every aspect of life
and you will be the **perfect embodiment of life**,
no matter who you are or what you do.

WE ARE the universe and **the universe is us.**
We are all **tiny specs** in a giant cosmic vacuum.

ENJOY THE RIDE,
and be **grateful** that you can.

www.ingramcontent.com/pod-product-compliance
Lightning Source LLC
Chambersburg PA
CBHW042021090426

42811CB00016B/1702